CHANDLER'S FORD -
YESTERDAY AND TODAY

by
Barbara Hillier
and
Gerald Ponting

Millers Dale Publications

Published 1998 by
Millers Dale Publications
7, Weavers Place
Chandler's Ford
Eastleigh, SO53 1TU

Cataloguing-in-Publication Data
A catalogue record for this book is available from the British Library

ISBN : 0 9517423 3 7

Printed by
Hobbs the Printers
Totton, Hants

Front Cover photograph :
Chandler's Ford Post Office, 1908 (see caption to photograph 57)

INTRODUCTION

"A 3500 year old cemetery has been discovered, laying in the path of an access road to a new housing development in Chandler's Ford". This quote from the *Southern Daily Echo* in 1997 described the latest piece of evidence to show that Bronze Age people lived in the area now known as Chandler's Ford. In 1882, a number of tumuli were excavated by the Hampshire Field and Archaeological Society. These ancient burial mounds were in the Hiltingbury area. Urns similar to those found in 1997 were taken for display in the Hartley Institute Museum in Southampton.

From the late sixteenth century, farms and farmworkers' cottages began to appear, scattered throughout an area of mixed woodland, heathland and wet meadow land – which at this time closely resembled parts of the New Forest. The farms were owned by large estates at Hursley, Otterbourne and North Stoneham, the three parishes to which different parts of the area belonged. This situation continued until 1897, when Chandler's Ford's first parish council was formed.

Ford Farm and Hiltonbury Farm were the earliest farms established. A number of Hiltonbury's farmworkers were housed in thatched cottages, built in the early seventeenth century in Ramalley Lane. This site became well-known for its annual "Merrie Fair", merries being the locally grown cherries which were harvested and sold as part of this social event. The fairs continued for two hundred years. It is recorded that Richard Cromwell, son of the Lord Protector, and his wife took part in the proceedings on at least one occasion, when they were living at Hursley Park House.

The road from Southampton to Winchester, as it passes through Chandler's Ford, follows very closely part of the old Roman road from Nursling to Winchester. It has always been a busy road, from the time of foot travellers and stage coaches to the present day. It was probably from the ford on this road, situated just to the north of the junction with Hursley Road, that the village got its name, although there were other fords in Hursley Road and in Leigh Road. "Chandler's" remains a mystery, as the spelling varies on different records and documents, until finally used with its current spelling on a map of 1789.

Three significant events of the nineteenth century began the change for Chandler's Ford from rural farming area to the residential community which we see today.

In 1847, the Salisbury branch of the London and South Western Railway was opened, making the area more accessible. Chandler's Ford acquired a station in November of that year. At first, it was little more than a "halt", and was used mainly by the Heathcote family of Hursley Park House, both for travel and for the delivery and sending of goods. In February 1848, Lady Selina Heathcote wrote in her diary, *"Sir William went up to Town from Chandler's Ford Station, now just opened"*. Again, on 31st July 1848, she records, *"Left by Express Train from Chandler's Ford for London at 9 a.m."*. The station grew over the years into a typical village station until its closure in 1969.

In the 1870's, it was discovered that the clay in this area, was particularly suitable for the making of bricks.. Brickyards were established in Common Road, in Oakmount Road and in the Scantabout area; but the largest one, reputed to be one of the biggest in the country, stretched from the railway towards Castle Lane, where the current Chandler's Ford Industrial Estate is situated. Bricks from this brickyard were used to build the Courts of Justice in The Strand in London. Inevitably, there was a need for housing in the area for the workers in the brickyards.

The third factor was the beginning of deliberate housing development. In 1892, Mrs. Mary Wallis sold land in Eastleigh for the building of the railway works. With the proceeds, she bought the Brownhill Estate in Chandler's Ford, which was then divided up and sold for building purposes. This led to the building of the late Victorian houses in Brownhill Road, Park Road, Valley Road and Hursley Road. Mr. and Mrs. Wallis built and lived at King's Court at Fryern Hill, now the Masonic Hall. Following these events, a number of other substantial properties came into existence, Chandler's Ford being promoted as a pleasant and healthy place in which to live.

The last fifty years of the nineteenth century saw Chandler's Ford take shape as a village, the population increasing from 250 at the time of the 1851 census to just over 1000 by 1900. The first Anglican church was erected in

Bournemouth Road in 1881, followed by the first nonconformist church in 1900. This was the Primitive Methodist Chapel, in the building which now houses the Age Concern Centre in Brownhill Road.

The first school was held in the building which was also the church, with Miss Isabel Laidlaw being the first headteacher. In 1893, the first purpose-built school was erected on a site on the corner of Bournemouth Road and School Lane. This was an all-age school with Mr. Bocking as its first headteacher.

The first Post Office was housed in the end building of a terrace opposite the Hut Hotel, to be succeeded in 1900 by a building on the corner of Hursley Road and Winchester Road. There were at least two small "general" shops, one in Oakmount Road and one on the corner of Common Road and Hursley Road. There was also a bakery at Fryern Hill, on the site occupied by Lloyds' Bank in the late 1990s.

The Halfway Inn was built in 1870. The Railway Hotel, now the Monk's Brook, followed in 1898. Hut Farm, which was situated behind the present Hendy Ford Showrooms, had a small building at the side, called the New Hut. Drinks were served here, and in 1894, it was succeeded by the Hut Hotel, quite a grand hostelry for its day, with accommodation for patrons and stabling for horses.

Horse-racing took place on the land of Titlark Farm, off Castle Lane, in the 1880's. By 1900 Chandler's Ford had its own football team.

Development between 1900 and 1939 was steady, with some farmland – and the grounds of some of the large houses – being sold for building development. This led to a population figure of just over 3000 by the time of World War II, with an appropriate increase in facilities to cope with the demands of a growing village. The general character of the place, however, remained very rural. Development since the war has been fast and extensive, to produce the large suburban community which we see today.

The photographs appearing on the left-hand pages of this book were taken between 1900 and 1975. Readers may find some to be familiar from Barbara's earlier books. With only a few exceptions, however, these pictures did not appear in either *"The Story of Chandler's Ford"* or *"Chandler's Ford - A Pictorial History"* . Gerald's photographs, which appear on the right-hand pages, were all taken in the spring and summer of 1998. Most were taken from the same spot as the originals. We hope our readers will enjoy "spotting the differences", for in some these are very obvious, while in others there are surprising similarities.

Acknowledgements

The photographs on the right-hand pages are all copyright Gerald Ponting. Those on the left-hand pages are part of Barbara Hillier's extensive collection. In most cases, the original photographer and present-day copyright holder, if any, are not known. Therefore, our sincere apologies to anyone whose permission should have been requested before publication.

Our grateful thanks to all those who donated or loaned the copies used to prepare this book :
Mr. Brown, Chandler's Ford Library, Mrs. B. Crumplin, *Eastleigh Weekly News*, Mrs. E.Hillier, Mrs. S. Holt, Mr. W. Munckton, Mr. L. Peach, Miss D. Wise – and for the cover photograph: Mr. R. Gibson.
Thanks also to Mrs. E. Hillier for her research in back copies of the *Eastleigh Weekly News*.

Contents

Note : only left-hand pages are listed. The photographs on the facing, right-hand, pages were all taken in 1998, mostly from the same positions.

Ford in Leigh Road, 1905 1

Opening the Leigh Road bridge, 1923 3

Hiltonbury Farmhouse, 1970 5

Hiltingbury Common, 1920s............................. 7

Heatherdean Road, 1940s................................... 9

Crescent Road, 1910 (Merdon Avenue).............. 11

Hiltingbury Lake, 1910 13

Hiltingbury Road / Lakewood Road, 1925 15

King's Court Lodge, 1905.................................. 17

King's Court, 1938.. 19

Brownhill Road, 1934 21

Southwood, 1910 (Woodhill School) 23

Sherborne House, 1934 25

Hursley Road, 1908... 27

Railway Hotel, 1910 (Monks Brook) 29

Station Lane, 1905 31

Chandler's Ford Station, 1950s.......................... 33

St Boniface Church, 1920 35

Children outside the church, 1910 37

Dr. and Mrs. Ritchie, 1908................................ 39

Children outside the Methodist Chapel, 1910...... 41

Congregational Church, 1950s............................ 43

Church of St Edward the Confessor, 1938.......... 45

Chandler's Ford School, 1900 47

Class at King's Road Infants School, 1920.......... 49

Southampton Road, 1910 (Bournemouth Road).. 51

The Parade, 1940s.. 53

Post Office, bottom of Hursley Road, 1910 55

Park Road / Common Road, 1920 57

Park Road / King's Road, 1950s 59

Hursley Road / Hiltingbury Road, 1950.............. 61

Lake Road, 1940s... 63

Hiltingbury Road / Malibres Road, 1950 65

The Hut Hotel, 1905... 67

The Mount Hotel, 1934 (King Rufus).................. 69

Shops at Fryern Hill, 1940s............................... 71

Chandler's Ford Library, 1950s 73

Mr. Munckton's Shop, 1934 75

South Hants Engineering Works, 1920s 77

House on site of Fryern Arcade, 1905................. 79

Carrefour under construction, 1974 (Asda)........ 81

1. Ford in Leigh Road, 1905. This shot of the Leigh Road ford is taken looking towards Chandler's Ford. As this is situated between the original settlements of Eastleigh and Chandler's Ford, it is not thought to be the ford which gave the area its name. (That was probably the ford which once existed in Winchester Road, just north of the present-day Central Precinct.) On the right of this picture can be seen the bridge by which foot travellers could cross the stream, but all vehicles had to go through the water until 1923.

2. Leigh Road, 1998. The railings on the right are the only indication to the casual observer that the road still crosses Monk's Brook at this point. By taking the left turn at the traffic lights, motorists now join the M3, which takes them towards Winchester, Basingstoke and London, or onto the A34 northwards to Newbury, Oxford and the Midlands. This section of the motorway was formed by upgrading the A33 Chandler's Ford by-pass, which had been first opened in 1967.

3. Opening the Leigh Road bridge, 14th December 1923. Work on constructing a bridge over the former ford began on 10th July 1923, road improvements having already taken place. Labourers were paid 31s. 10d. (equivalent to £1.59) for a 44-hour week. Work was offered to as many unemployed men as possible. On 14th December, after a luncheon attended by a number of representatives from the surrounding area, Mr. J. E. Willis Fleming, J.P., cut the ribbon to mark the official opening of the bridge. It had cost £16,500 to build.

4. Motorway bridge, 1998. Unlike most of the modern photographs appearing in this book, this one is not taken from the same spot as that appearing opposite. Instead, we are standing on the pavement of the Leigh Road bridge, looking downstream to where the brook passes under the M3. In this direction, the motorway leads to Southampton, with slip roads onto the M27 eastbound for Portsmouth and the M27 westbound for the New Forest and Bournemouth.

5. Hiltonbury Farmhouse, 1970. The original section of the farmhouse dates back to the sixteenth century and so is one of the oldest buildings in Chandler's Ford. It has a number of nineteenth century additions which have a style similar to other buildings which belonged to the Hursley Park Estates at the time. The distinctive chimneys are a good example. When Richard Cromwell, son of Oliver, owned the Hursley estates, the farmer at Hiltonbury was Mr. Ellis – who led a rebellion against the Lord of the Manor for raising farm rents. Ellis was imprisoned in Winchester Prison for cutting down oak, ash and apple trees to repair gates and buildings which were in a ruinous condition.

6. Hiltonbury Farmhouse, 1998. Today the farmhouse is a Listed Building – and a popular public house. The former farmland around the building is now largely occupied by the North Millers Dale housing estate, although some of the damper lower-lying land is managed by the Hampshire Wildlife Trust as Flexford Nature Reserve. It ceased to be a working farm in 1976, the last farmer having been Mr. John Vining, who had farmed there since 1946. He had taken over from his uncle, Mr. George Beattie, who had succeeded his father, Mr. Simon Beattie. *He* had occupied the farm from 1887.

7. Hiltingbury Common, 1920s. Mrs Bess Crumplin has lived all her life in a bungalow in Hursley Road. This photograph shows her sister Helen gathering heather on Hiltingbury Common. The Common was situated on the north side of what is now Hiltingbury Road and was an area of heathland, supporting nightjars, stonechats and other heathland species.

8. Sycamore Avenue and Ashdown Road, 1998. Hiltingbury Common was developed in the 1960s with houses, bungalows, flats and shops. This view is taken from Sycamore Avenue, looking across an open area towards housing on Ashdown Road.

HEATHERDEAN. ROAD
HILTINGBURY. ESTATE
CHANDLERS FORD

9. Heatherdean Road, 1940s. This photograph shows Heatherdean Road at its junction with Thorold Road, looking across to the start of Grosvenor Road – then an area of mixed woodland with many silver birch and sweet chestnut trees. In the run-up to D-Day in 1944, this area was the temporary home of an estimated 10,000 troops. Except for Hursley Road and the main Southampton-Winchester road, every road and track was blocked by army transport vehicles. The few people then living in the Hiltingbury area needed official passes to leave and return to their homes.

10. Heatherdene Road, 1998. The same scene over half a century later. Note the slight change from the original spelling. Since the Second World War, this part of Hiltingbury has developed into a quiet residential area with mature gardens, many of which still contain silver birch and sweet chestnut trees.

11. Crescent Road, 1910. The name of this road was changed from Crescent Road to Merdon Avenue in 1932, when Chandler's Ford first became part of the Borough of Eastleigh – which already had a road of that name. This scene is just beyond the junction with Park Road, looking towards a track in the distance, leading off to the left, which is now Oakwood Road. Behind the hedge on the left was a large house with the unusual name of Roo.

12. Merdon Avenue, 1998. The pine trees are still there, but Roo has gone, replaced by smaller, more modern houses. The 'wheelie-bin', green to take 'recyclables', is a sign that the twentieth century has moved on by nearly ninety years.

13. Hiltingbury Lake, 1910. The existing lake at Hiltingbury is the remaining one of a former series of lakes which may have originated as ancient fish-ponds. There is even a small possibility that this was part of the fishery recorded for Otterbourne in the Domesday Book. Earlier in the twentieth century, during severe winters, the ice on the lake was sometimes thick enough for skating parties to be organised.

14. Hiltingbury Lake, 1998. The Countryside Service of Eastleigh Borough Council now maintains the lake and the surrounding area. It is a pleasant place to sit or stroll or fish. The lake, with its surrounding woodland, supports a range of birds, mammals and insect life throughout the year.

A Woodland Road Chandlers Ford.

T.H. B 22

15. Hiltingbury Road / Lakewood Road, 1925. This photograph has been taken looking westwards along the tree-lined stony track which was Hiltingbury Road in those days. The motor-cycle-and-sidecar, probably belonging to the photographer commissioned to take this post-card view, is parked near the crossroads with Lakewood Road. The trees on the left conceal a view down to Hiltingbury Lake. In the 1930s, the *Eastleigh Weekly News* recorded that, in this area, *"nightingales were heard singing by night and by day"*.

16. Hiltingbury Road / Lakewood Road, 1998. There is still a wooded area on the left, leading down to the lake, but the right-hand side of the road has been developed with housing. Sadly, in 1998, no nightingales have been recorded !

17. King's Court Lodge, 1905. This was the lodge at the main entrance gate to King's Court (see photograph 19). The person standing outside the lodge was a Mr. Young. The name 'King's Court' is still decipherable on the gateposts.

18. King's Court Restaurant, 1998. In the 1930s, the lodge was extended and became a restaurant, initially known as King's Court Roadhouse. It no longer acts as a lodge and visitors to King's Court itself now need to turn into the adjacent road, a modern development called The Hillway.

19. King's Court, 1938. Mr. and Mrs. Wallis built King's Court in 1894, from the proceeds of land in Eastleigh which they had sold for the building of the railway works. This photograph was taken 44 years later when the house came up for sale by auction. The suggested price was £2,200 and part of the sale description read – *"Delightful hall with galleried staircase, Gent's cloakroom, four well-proportioned reception rooms, thirteen bed and dressing rooms, two bathrooms, well-arranged offices. Electric light. Gas and water. Central heating. Main drainage. 2½ acres of garden with tennis court."*

20. The Masonic Hall, 1998. King's Court was a school for a short time in the 1930s, while during the Second World War it housed the offices of the White Star Line, which had moved out of Southampton due to the bombing. Today it has become the Masonic Hall. The distinctive point on the corner tower has been removed for safety reasons and the verdant approach replaced by a car-park, but visitors are still greeted by the *"delightful hall with galleried staircase"* described in 1938.

21. Brownhill Road, 1934. Here we are looking westwards and downhill, with Fryern Hill behind us. In the previous year, work had been completed on improving the surface of the road, constructing pavements and installing gas street lamps. The large house which can be seen amongst the trees at the bottom of the hill is Fryern. This was owned by Mr. Thurston, after whom Thurston Close is named.

22. Brownhill Road, 1998. Note the modern electric street lamp on the same spot as the old gas lamp. The bungalows on the left were built during the late 1930s, when much of the land which had formerly been part of the King's Court grounds was sold for housing development.

23. Southwood, 1910. Southwood, situated in Brownhill Road near its junction with Park Road, was built as a school just one hundred years earlier than the photograph opposite, in 1898. In 1904, when the Principal was Mrs. Carter, the school performed a concert in aid of the Building Fund for the new St. Boniface Church.

24. Woodhill School, 1998. Today, Southwood forms part of Woodhill School, a preparatory day school for boys and girls aged 3 – 11 years. The school also occupies the adjacent house, Connaught Lodge, which for many years prior to the Second World War was the home of the Sandell family.

25. Sherborne House, 1934. Mrs. Wise was born in Sherborne, Dorset in 1880, the second of six children – her father was the headmaster of Sherborne Abbey School. In 1932, she was looking for a suitable location to open her own independent school. At the suggestion of a friend and with the support of the vicar, the Rev. Harold Fryer, she decided on Chandler's Ford. The first building that her school occupied was Dunottar, now no. 12 Park Road. In 1934, the school moved to the house shown in the photograph, The Wattles, in Lakewood Road.

26. Sherborne House, 1998. Mrs. Wise died in 1964 and her daughter Dorothy succeeded as headteacher. Her other daughter, Nancy, also taught at the school until her death in 1967. Miss Dorothy Wise retired in 1984, after over fifty years with the school. Today, this independent preparatory school is run by Mr. and Mrs. Clewer, but it has kept the same name, recalling the Wise family's connections with the town of Sherborne. The photograph shows the modern extensions to the school building.

HURSLEY ROAD, CHANDLERSFORD

27. Hursley Road, 1908. Here we are looking northwards along Hursley Road at the point where it crosses the Monk's Brook. Before this bridge was constructed, in the latter years of the nineteenth century, there was a ford at this point. The sign of the Railway Hotel is just visible behind the bushes. In 1909, the small building on the right of the photograph was opened as a Reading and Recreation Room.

28. Hursley Road, 1998. Today, there is a much clearer view of the hotel, renamed The Monks Brook since Chandler's Ford station became defunct. The actual Brook still flows beneath the bridge at this point. Until work was carried out on its banks in the 1960s, the road often suffered severe flooding in wet winters.

29. The Railway Hotel, 1910. The hotel was built in 1898 to provide accommodation and refreshment for passengers travelling to and from Chandler's Ford by train (see Introduction). At the time that this photograph was taken, Park Road was a rough track and a tall tree was growing at its junction with Hursley Road.

30. The Monks Brook, 1998. The hotel has changed its name, tarmac now inevitably dominates the picture, and traffic bollards stand where the tree once grew.

Chandlersford   Mentor&Co

31. Station Lane, 1905. Before the railway was constructed in 1847, the road to Hursley diverged from the Southampton - Winchester road along what is now Station Lane. By standing outside Fortune Court in Hursley Road, the route of the old road can clearly be seen. This view, looking in the opposite direction from Station Lane, shows the station buildings and, in the distance, the newly built St. Boniface Church.

32. Station Lane, 1998. The station has gone, at the bottom of Station Lane there is a car park for shoppers at The Parade, and the distant view is obscured by trees and bushes. The house on the left, seen in both pictures, is called Fernvale and was built at the beginning of the twentieth century.

33. Chandler's Ford Station, 1950s. The station was opened in November 1847. The line was double track and carried a regular service between Eastleigh and Romsey, until the closure of the station in 1969. In the nineteenth century, a single-track railway was constructed from the station through the brickyard which stretched as far as Castle Lane; this was used for the transport of bricks.

34. Railway track, 1998. The railway is now single track and carries mainly goods traffic. As this book goes to press, the station site, long a derelict eyesore, is being redeveloped with sixteen two-bedroomed apartments. However, the platforms of the former station still exist – will passenger rail traffic ever return to Chandler's Ford ?

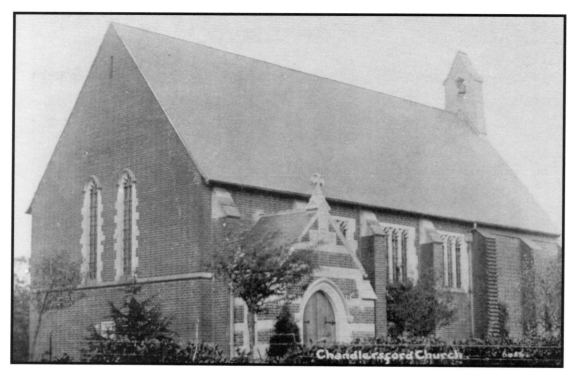

Chandlersford Church

35. St. Boniface Church, 1920. St. Boniface Church in Hursley Road was dedicated by the Bishop of Winchester on Tuesday October 4th 1904. It replaced an earlier Anglican church situated on Bournemouth Road. The first service in the new church was led by the Rev. Vere Awdrey, Vicar of Ampfield – and father of the creator of Thomas the Tank Engine. The church had cost £3,400 to build and had seating for 230 people.

36. St. Boniface Church, 1998. This picture, taken from a different direction, shows a number of changes to the building. In 1929, a chancel was added to the church, an organ was installed and the belfry was moved to the other end of the roof. The St. Boniface Centre was added in 1987, being dedicated on 28th February. It provides modern accommodation for various meetings and activities, with the former church porch moved through ninety degrees to act as an entrance to both the Church and the Centre.

37. Children outside the Church, 1910. We do not know the reason for this gathering of children or why they were photographed – but there would have been a much larger gathering on 5th October in the same year. On that day, the school was given a half-holiday to see the first wedding to be held in the church. Mr. Francis Dudley of St. Albans married Miss Ethel Hornsby of Chandler's Ford.

38. Houses opposite the Church, 1998. The same houses can be identified as in the photograph taken 88 years earlier. Reading from right to left, these houses in Hursley Road were originally called Rotherwood, Conisburgh, Altrest and Oakleigh. Oakleigh was the St. Boniface vicarage for a while, until the new Vicarage was built on the opposite side of the road, next-door to the church.

39. Dr. and Mrs. Ritchie, 1908. Dr. Edward Duguid Ritchie was a popular General Practitioner in Chandler's Ford for a period of fifteen years, from 1897 till 1912. He took a keen interest in village and church activities, being Honorary Treasurer of Chandler's Ford Football Club, choirmaster, lay reader and Secretary of the Winchester Diocesan Choral Union.

40. The Ritchie Memorial Hall, 1998. When Dr. Ritchie died in 1912, Mrs. Ritchie gave £700 for the building of a village hall in his memory. Situated next to St. Boniface Church, the Ritchie Hall was opened on 16th April 1914. The Community Centre building has now been added to it, forming a complex of rooms suitable for a wide variety of meetings and functions.

41. Children outside the Methodist Chapel, 1910. This chapel in Brownhill Road was opened in November 1900. It was built by Mr. Charles Mitchell's building firm of Woodfalls, near Salisbury, but the bricks were all made in Chandler's Ford brickworks. Including the purchase of the land, the chapel cost a total of £400. Initially, it had seating for 120 people, but it was extended in 1937. It ceased to be a chapel in 1957, when new premises were opened in Winchester Road.

42. Age Concern Centre, 1998. A new Methodist Church was built in 1969, next to the all-purpose premises which had been built in 1957. In 1993, the buildings were extended and completely re-furbished. Meanwhile, the former chapel, seen here, became the Age Concern Centre. A pair of semi-detached houses standing next to it were demolished when the car park for Safeway, seen in the foreground of this picture, was constructed in the 1970s.

43. Congregational Church, 1950s. In 1923, a retired Congregational minister, the Rev. Daniel Lloyd Jones, came to live at Pencoed in Brownhill Road. This was situated on the site of the present-day Brownhill Close. With Rev. Jones' leadership and enthusiasm, funds were raised for the construction of a Congregational Church in King's Road. This was opened on 17th October 1929, with seating for 300. Its first minister was the Rev. Reginald Dennis Cooper.

44. United Reformed Church, 1998. In 1972, the Congregational and Presbyterian Churches in England combined to become the United Reformed Church. Locally, the church in King's Road undertook a substantial building and refurbishment programme. In 1997, it appointed its first lady minister, the Rev. Maz Allen.

CHURCH OF ST. EDWARD THE CONFESSOR.   CHANDLERS FORD.

45. Church of St. Edward the Confessor (Roman Catholic), 1938. Mr. Edward Christian was born at Malvern in 1858. In 1893, he married Helen Ringgold, daughter of Mr. and Mrs. John Moylan Thomas of Philadelphia. In 1904, he bought Otterbourne House and became Lord of the Manor of Otterbourne. He died on 3rd April 1934 and was buried in Otterbourne churchyard. His widow, a Roman Catholic, provided the funds for the building of the Church of St. Edward the Confessor on Winchester Road. It was consecrated on 10th March 1938.

46. Church of St. Edward the Confessor, 1998. This modern photograph, from a slightly different angle, shows the extension to the original building, which was added in 1988.

Chandlersford Schools.

47. Chandler's Ford School, 1900. This school was built in 1893 on Bournemouth Road – which was then known as Southampton Road – at its junction with what became known as School Lane. It was an all-age school, for pupils from 5-14, and its first headmaster was Mr. Bocking. When an Infants' School was opened in King's Road in 1908, this became the school for the older pupils, covering the age range 9-14. It closed in 1939 after the North End Secondary School was built in Leigh Road. (This was the fore-runner of Thornden School, Thornden being simply an anagram of 'North End'.)

48. School Lane / Bournemouth Road junction, 1998. Mr. William Selwood began his plant hire and engineering business in the old school building, shortly after the Second World War. As the business grew, new premises were built and the old school was demolished in 1984. So 'School Lane' no longer has a school and forms the spine road of the Chandler's Ford Industrial Estate, which occupies the land where the brickfields were once situated.

49. Class at King's Road Infants School, 1920. This school opened in 1908. In 1996, a new extension was officially opened by the Lord Lieutenant of Hampshire. The children presented a bouquet to Mrs. Sybil Holt, the oldest former pupil present at the ceremony. She is one of the group in this 1920 photograph, taken when she was eight years old.

50. Pupils at Chandler's Ford Infants School, 1998. This group of Year One pupils, in their smart uniforms, was taken in front of the recently painted wall of the school hall. This is very colourful and stimulates much interest, both for those in the school and for passers-by. The school also has an ambitious plan for the enhancement of the school grounds. No such exciting additions to the school environment were thought to be desirable in 1920 !

51. Southampton Road, 1910. This view was taken looking northwards towards the Hut Hotel, which can be seen in the distance on the right of the road. On the left is St. Boniface House, which is where the first Sunday School in Chandler's Ford was held in the 1880s, led by Mr. Ingram and his daughter.

52. Bournemouth Road, 1998. The same road, the same spot, but a different name, most of the buildings hidden by vegetation – and certainly no safety for the photographer to stand in the middle of the road to take this shot – or for a cyclist to pose for the photographer ! However, the Hut Hotel, St. Boniface House and many of the other features to be seen in 1910 are still there, behind the trees and bushes. The coming of cable television has scarred the pavement.

53. The Parade, 1940s. This row of shops in Bournemouth Road was built in the 1930s. The businesses operating in The Parade in its early years were – chemist, sweet-shop, Cooperative, butcher, baker, radio and electrical service, National Provincial Bank, grocer, ladies hairdresser, wine and spirits shop, ladies outfitter and fishmonger. The building in the distance, on the corner of Hursley Road and Winchester Road, housed the offices and showroom of the Gas Company at this time.

54. The Parade, 1998. Of the original list of trades, only a butcher remains, although today's newsagent sells sweets and there is a gents' hairdressers. Unimaginable in the 1930s or 1940s, there is also a pizza take-away and a Balti take-away. The number of motor vehicles has increased vastly, despite the fact that this ceased to be the main route between Winchester and Southampton over thirty years ago. The Gas Company building has long gone (see pictures 55 and 56).

POST OFFICE CHANDLERS FORD 102

55. Post Office, bottom of Hursley Road, 1910. This building, occupied by the Gas Company in the 1940s, was built as a Post Office in 1900. (See also front cover photograph.) The post-master at the time of this photograph was Mr. Tuersley, who started the first Boy Scout troop in Chandler's Ford in 1911. Like his father and five brothers, he had spent some time in the Regular Army. In 1900, in the final years of Victoria's reign, his father had received the following communication from Buckingham Palace – *"It has been brought to the Queen's notice that not only did you serve for over 21 years under the Colours, but at the present time you have six sons in the Army. I am commanded by the Queen to express to you the satisfaction with which Her Majesty has learnt of this almost unique instance of continued and exemplary service in one family".*

56. Central Precinct roundabout, 1998. The old post office building was demolished in 1984, when the road junction was widened and the roundabout constructed. No place for leaning on your bicycle in the middle of the road (as in the photograph opposite) in the 1990s ! By the way, have you seen him somewhere before ?

57. Park Road / Common Road, 1920. This view is looking south down Park Road, with the corner of Common Road in the left foreground. The three houses on the right were called The Pines, The Brambles and Rufus Lodge. Further along Common Road, just beyond the point where the children are standing, was Chandler's Ford's first laundry. The 'Snowball Laundry' had begun as a family business in 1898.

58. Park Road / Common Road, 1998. The three houses remain and have retained the same names. The laundry building was destroyed by fire in 1958. After rebuilding, it continued as Chanex Laundry until it became part of Initial Services. It has been replaced, in this decade, by a small housing development, The Maples.

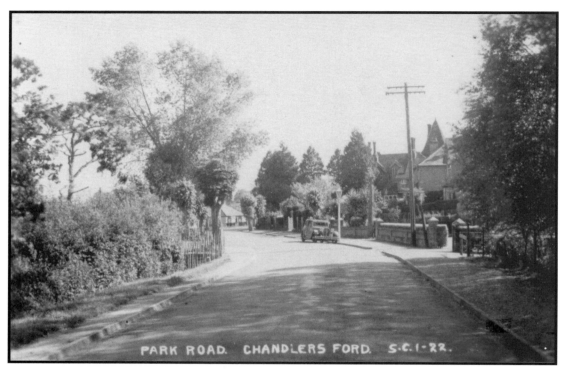

PARK ROAD. CHANDLERS FORD. S.C.1-22.

59. Park Road / King's Road, 1950s. A little further south than the last two pictures, this is looking towards Park Road's junction with King's Road. At this time, there were no houses on the left and the brook flowed on either side of King's Road. Children on their way to what was then the Primary School often played in the brook till the last possible moment, thus arriving at school in a somewhat wet and dishevelled condition.

60. Park Road / King's Road, 1998. The left-hand side of Park Road has been developed since the 1950s and the brook has been closed in. The footpath known as Church Path, leaving Park Road on the right, leads through to Hursley Road. Those who spent their childhood in this area in the 1940s and 1950s will remember Mrs. Bailey who lived with an assortment of livestock in a thatched cottage along this path. Rumour had it that she was 'a gentlewoman who had come down in the world', but children found her a rather fearsome person and passed by her cottage as quickly as possible.

61. Hursley Road / Hiltingbury Road, 1950. A remarkably traffic-free view to those who know this busy junction today ! The Chandler's Ford cricket ground was situated behind the bushes on the right of the picture. The signpost points left along Hiltingbury Road to the 'No. 17 Families' Camp', which was established in the woods to the north of this road a few years after the Second World War and continued till 1956. This was a temporary home for Army Services families, complete with a school for the children, a Brownie Pack and a Guide Company. To the south of Hiltingbury Road there was a camp for Polish refugees, which was disbanded in 1957. However, in one corner of the cemetery in Pine Road, there is a little group of graves marked by crosses with Polish names.

62. Hursley Road / Hiltingbury Road, 1998. The scene here is still tree-lined but there are traffic lights at the busy cross-roads. The development of more housing at Knightwood Park in the late 1990s is generating even more traffic. Residents of the North Millers Dale housing estate (built in the 1980s over former farmland and the cricket pitch) frequently complain of the lack of a pedestrian phase at these lights, making a walk to the shops in Hiltingbury and Ashdown Roads a dangerous exercise.

63. Lake Road, 1940s. Lake Road forms a crescent between Hiltingbury Road and Kingsway; most of the houses lining the left-hand side of the road date from the 1920s. Formerly, the road existed as a footpath giving access to the lake (pictures 13 and 14) which is behind the trees on the right of the road.

64. Lake Road, 1998. Today, the houses are almost concealed by mature trees and bushes. The scene looks almost as peaceful as that taken over half a century earlier – although visitors to the lake often use this road to park their cars.

65. Hiltingbury Road / Malibres Road, 1950. The photographer is facing westwards, with the Winchester Road junction not far behind him. The houses seen here were built in the late 1920s and early 1930s. The first road leading off to the right is Malibres Road. In the twelfth and thirteenth centuries, the Manor of Boyatt belonged to Waverley Abbey (near Farnham, Surrey). In 1219, Adam, Abbott of Waverley, leased a dwelling, eleven acres of land and two acres of meadow to one Nicholas Malherbe, after whom this area and later Malibres Road was named.

66. Hiltingbury Road, 1998. Since the building of the North Millers Dale and Valley Park developments (and now Knightwood Park) and particularly with the construction of the Pitmore interchange (M3 junction 13), Hiltingbury Road has become a busy thoroughfare. Traffic calming measures, both here and in the parallel Hocombe Road, have been discussed at length but, at the time of going to press, have not yet materialised.

67. The Hut Hotel, 1905. This hotel was built in 1894 on what was then the Southampton Road. It provided refreshment and accommodation for travellers – and stabling for their horses.

68. The Hut Hotel, 1998. Today, The Hut is part of the Beefeater chain of pub-restaurants. In 1997, the oak tree which had stood at the front of the hotel for over one hundred years was found to be unsafe. Although it had to be felled, the stump of the trunk remains a feature of The Hut's frontage.

69. The Mount Hotel, 1934. The Mount, situated on the corner of Merdon Avenue and Winchester Road, began life as a private house. By 1915, it had become a boarding house and by 1923 a private hotel. At the time that this photograph was taken, visitors could stay at the hotel for 14 shillings (70p) per day or £4.10s. (£4.50) per week - *"no extras. Breakfasts, luncheons, teas and dinners served to non-residents. Poultry and eggs from our own farm"*. In the same year, 1934, the hotel served two very special 'non-residents'. The King and Queen of Siam (now Thailand) were on holiday in England. On a journey from London to Bournemouth, they stopped at The Mount for afternoon tea. They were particularly impressed by the beautiful English garden.

70. The King Rufus, 1998. With the present-day trend of renaming public houses and hotels, The Mount, after a period as Hanrahan's, is now The King Rufus. This name acknowledges the local legend concerning the body of King William II, 'William Rufus'. He was killed (by accident, murder or conspiracy?) while hunting in the New Forest on 2nd August 1100. The fatal arrow had been fired by Sir Walter Tyrell. According to the legend, the King's body was found by a charcoal burner, William Purkess, and taken by him to Winchester on a cart, passing through Chandler's Ford on the way. This also explains the origin of several local street names, including Kingsway, King's Road, Tyrell Road and Rufus Close (but Purkess Close was named from another Mr. Purkess, who lived much more recently).

71. Shops at Fryern Hill, 1940s. This row of shops was built in the 1930s, about ten years before the photograph was taken. They seemed to attract traders with names appropriate to their businesses – Trims the hairdresser and House the estate agent ! Fernhill Cottages, beyond the shops, had been built in 1882. Beyond them is The Halfway Inn, built in 1870.

72. Shops at Fryern Hill, 1998. Although none of the original businesses remain, hair is still styled here by Trevor Mitchell and properties may be bought and sold through Fox and Son. Typically of the latter twentieth century, each of these is a branch of a larger organisation, not an independent trader. Only three of the six Fernhill Cottages remain private residences. The Halfway Inn still marks the halfway point between Southampton and Winchester – but today it is less an inn for travellers, attracting customers by such 1990s events as karaoke nights and the screening of satellite sports programmes.

73. Chandler's Ford Library, 1950s. In the 1940s and 1950s, Chandler's Ford's library was situated in this estate agents' premises at Fryern Hill. It then moved to one of the shops in Hursley Road, opposite the Monk's Brook. Its final home before the new library was built was in a temporary building situated next to F. H. Dean and Son's shop in Hursley Road.

74. Chandler's Ford Library, 1998. The new branch of the Hampshire Library Service was built at Fryern Hill in 1983 and now loans not only books of all descriptions but also cassette tapes, CDs and videos. The group of shops on either side of the approach to the library from Winchester Road is known as The Mall. This development was officially opened in 1988 by Lord and Lady Romsey of Broadlands House.

75. Mr Munckton's shop, 1934. In the early years of the twentieth century, this shop at the corner of Oakmount Road and Winchester Road was a baker's which also served teas. By 1934, when this photograph was taken, it was a grocer's, with Mr. Munckton as its proprietor.

76. Lloyds Bank, 1998. When this photograph was taken, Lloyds Bank had occupied these premises for only a few months, having previously had a branch in The Parade. Above the bank are the offices of Mowlem Southern Civil Engineering. Chandler's Ford has a tenuous connection with the Mowlem family of Swanage, founders of the Mowlem organisation. Mr. Burt lived and worked as a stonemason in Hursley Road for 34 years. He was the nephew of Sir John Mowlem and was one of the workmen who helped to fashion the Great Globe which can still be seen in the Durlston Country Park near Swanage.

77. South Hants Engineering Works, 1920s. This garage was built in the 1920s and was one of Chandler's Ford's first garages. Its proprietor was Mr. J. F. Gorst. In 1928, the Parish Council agreed on a speed limit of 10 m.p.h. on the main Southampton – Winchester road, concern having been expressed about the speed of motor vehicles passing through the village! The building in the background, also dating from the 1920s, housed two shops, a baker's and a haberdashers and ladies' dress shop. One customer remembers buying a summer dress there in 1935, costing five shillings (25p).

78. Safeway Store, 1998. In the 1970s, the garage was demolished and the Safeway supermarket was built on the site. Although small by the standard of supermarkets in the 1990s, this is a very busy store with a large turnover. The yew tree in the car park behind the store, now shading a trolley park, marks the position of a blacksmith's which was still active in 1920. The former dress shop is now a popular greengrocer's, while the former baker's sells mobile phones.

79. House which became the Wide-Awake Café, 1905. This house formerly stood where cars now enter the Fryern Arcade car-park. The family in the photograph is the Savory family, the last people to use this as a private residence. Between the wars, the house was altered and extended before opening as the Wide-Awake Café - which became very well-known in the locality.

80. The Fryern Arcade, 1998. This group of shops, now conveniently close to Safeway's, the library and banks, was officially opened on 4th July 1967. The ceremony was performed by the Mayor of Eastleigh, Councillor A. J. Griffin, accompanied by Monsieur Marius Faisse, the Mayor of Villeneuve-St-Georges, Eastleigh's twin town.

81. Carrefour under construction, 1974. In 1937, this site had been a refugee camp when some 4,000 Basque children, escaping from the Spanish Civil War, arrived in Southampton on the liner *Havana*. In 1974, a French company, Carrefour, built one of Britain's very first hypermarkets here. An aerial photograph of the development even featured in a late 1970s school geography textbook as 'the shape of things to come'.

82. Building an extension to the Asda store, 1998. Before supermarkets became as widespread as they are in the late '90s, the Carrefour store attracted shoppers from a very wide area. For a brief spell, it became a Gateway store, then was taken over and re-furbished as part of the Asda chain, one of the 'big four'. In 1998, the builders are at work again, constructing a major extension onto the front of the store.

In this book, we hope that we have given you a series of glimpses of how Chandler's Ford has changed and grown over the twentieth century. It seems appropriate to end with one of the best-known buildings in the area, again undergoing a major change. No doubt the twenty-first century has many more changes in store for our local community.

Bibliography

Chandler's Ford United Reformed Church – the First Fifty Years (1979)

Dalton, Joan :
Two plus 75 – a Story of Guiding in Chandler's Ford (1997)

Eastleigh Weekly News (1898-1944)

Hegan, Margot :
St. Boniface and St. Martin in the Wood (1993)

Hillier, Barbara J. :
The Story of Chandler's Ford (1984)

Hillier, Barbara J. :
Chandler's Ford – A Pictorial History (1994)

Otterbourne Parish Council :
A Portrait of Otterbourne (1982)

Peach, D. L. :
The Diary of Selina, Lady Heathcote (1984)

St. Edward the Confessor's Church, Chandler's Ford, 1938-1988

Wise, Dorothy :
Sherborne House School (1985)

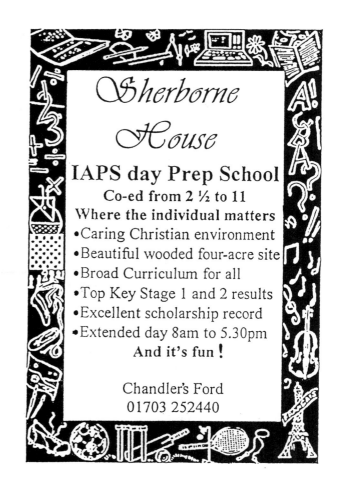

About the Authors

Barbara Hillier was born in Chandler's Ford and attended Chandler's Ford Primary School and Barton Peveril Grammar School, Eastleigh. She trained as a teacher at Rolle College, Exmouth and later gained a Diploma in Advanced Educational Studies at the University of Southampton. She has taught in Secondary, Primary and Special Schools in Southampton, Romsey, Eastleigh and Basingstoke, specialising in pupils with special educational needs. Latterly, prior to her early retirement, she was a Teacher Adviser for pupils with learning difficulties with Hampshire's Inspection and Advisory Support Service. Barbara has a particular interest in local history - her two previous books are listed in the bibliography - and has also researched and recorded the history of her family. She is a member of the Chandler's Ford Methodist Church, of which four of her great-grandparents were founder members. She chairs the local committee of the Hampshire Wildlife Trust and is the voluntary warden of Flexford Nature Reserve.

Gerald Ponting was born in Breamore, near Fordingbridge, and attended Bishop Wordsworth's School, Salisbury. Following study at the Universities of Southampton and Leicester, Gerald's career as a Biology Teacher took him first to Suffolk. Here he began to take an interest in local history, researching and writing the history of Kesgrave, near Ipswich. During ten years in the Outer Hebrides, he wrote a number of books about the Standing Stones of Callanish and lectured on the topic in the U.S.A. He received a British Archaeological Award for researches at Callanish. On returning to Hampshire, he taught at The Burgate School, Fordingbridge, for eight years, until his early retirement. Gerald is now a Blue Badge Tourist Guide and a free-lance writer, photographer and lecturer; he has lived in Chandler's Ford for the past eleven years. With Anthony Light, he has written and published ten books and booklets on local history in the Fordingbridge area – with more in the pipeline. He is enthusiastic about the use of computers in photography, local history and publishing and is very pleased that this is his first book supplied to the printers entirely on disc.